How To Have A Great Relationship:

96 Tips For Turning A Healthy Relationship Into The Perfect Relationship

By Maree Crosbie

How To Have A Great Relationship: 96 Tips For Turning A Healthy Relationship Into The Perfect Relationship
ISBN: 1453823743
EAN- 13: 9781453823743

Thank you to my wonderful husband Nicholas for 20 years of true love and companionship. I look forward to sharing many more.

"When something is missing in your life, it usually turns out to be someone." - Robert Brault

1

People respond to honesty. In a world where people are often faced with scams and lies, honesty is a priority. The relationships you form with honesty as a foundation will be strong and powerful.

Apologize if you're in the wrong.

2

If you're wrong about anything or do something that offends or hurts someone, admit it. Everyone makes mistakes; after all, we're all human. People respect you more if you admit your mistakes and apologize. Respect strengthens your relationships.

3

First and foremost, if you want to build a relationship that's positive, passionate, and withstanding, you need to give 100% of yourself. This is one of the most important things for success, not only in your relationships, but life in general. There's no "50/50" when it comes to giving in a relationship. It's almost impossible to receive from your partner if you don't give in return.

Focus on loving your partner.

4

In nurturing a positive relationship, your main focus should be on simply loving your partner. Show your love in both your words and actions, in all you say and do. The expression "actions speak louder than words," is definitely true when it comes to a relationship. However, your partner still wants to hear you say, "I love you."

Use charitable acts.

5

The things you do for your partner make a difference in your relationship. When you love someone, acts of kindness toward him or her come naturally. No action should be done just because you feel obligated to do it. The things you do for your partner should be done because you want to do them.

Respect your partner.

6

Always respect your partner in every way to build a lasting and positive relationship with them. Respect is an important building block of any relationship. Respect your partner not only in a physical sense, but also mentally, emotionally, and spiritually as well.

Build a strong friendship.

7

Your romantic relationship needs to have the stability and deep roots that come from a strong friendship. With a meaningful friendship as its basis, your relationship becomes stronger and more lasting. When you work hard to construct a strong friendship, you can be assured that your relationship is ready to weather whatever life may throw at you in the future.

Show your gratitude.

8

If you love your partner, then you're obviously grateful for them. However, you need to learn to express your inner feelings. Your partner needs to know that you're grateful. You can show gratitude by being more open in your conversations or by taking loving actions like buying gifts or suggesting ideas for quality time. Also, remember the words: "Thank you!"

Incorporate more fun into the relationship.

9

You two may have separate ideas of what fun is, but try doing things together that you both enjoy. It doesn't have to be anything big and extravagant, just try to find something simple, yet exciting. The key is to do something where you both won't know exactly what to expect. This adds that "special spice" to the relationship and helps stave off boredom.

Go out of your way.

10

Yes, going out of your way for your partner may take some extra work, but it'll be worth it! Decide to make a grand gesture for your partner. Do this out of the blue and your partner will really see that you care. For example, you could throw them a party or take care of something that you know they don't like doing.

Do activities they want to do.

11

By making the sacrifice to do something you're not all that interested in, it'll make your partner feel loved and honored. Of course, there'll be interests you share, but make it a point to join in for an activity they really enjoy more than you do.

Keep their needs in mind.

12

As the years go by, it's so easy to fall into patterns and restricted comfort zones, but you mustn't forget about your partner's needs. If they enjoy an extra hug every once in awhile, go give them a hug. If they like to talk about feelings and plans, sit with them and talk.

Say: "I love you" regularly.

13

It seems that you can never say these three simple words enough. Say it, text it, email it, record it, show it. Do what you have to just to remind your partner of your true feelings. This little phrase helps communication, lightens the mood, and fosters a more loving relationship for many years to come.

Listen actively.

14

While it's important to express your own feelings, it's also critical that you truly listen to your partner's feelings. When you actively listen, you'll begin to understand your partner in a new, deeper way. They'll also feel loved because they'll see you being attentive and they'll feel like their thoughts and feelings matter.

Support their ideas.

15

When you agree with your partner's ideas, make sure that you fully support them in both words and actions. This feeling of support will help your partner feel loved.

Go out of your way.

16

Remember at the beginning of your relationship how you would go out of your way to make your partner extra happy? Make these efforts again! It'll surprise your partner and be a reminder about how much you love them. It doesn't have to be an everyday thing, but everyone deserves a little "above and beyond" treatment!

Be considerate.

17

Sometimes your partner is the only one who will allow you to be blunt and abrupt. It's important to vent, but remember to act considerate around your partner as much as you can.

Spend time alone together.

18

Everyone is busy, but you need to make the extra effort to have alone time together. It's still important to make dates with each other and do things you've never done before.

Show affection.

19

There are certainly ways to show your affection for your partner beyond bedroom activities. Show your love for each other with gentle touches and hugs. Snuggle together on the couch and just enjoy the closeness.

Seek adventure.

20

Everyone has his or her own definition of adventure. You and your partner may even find different things adventurous. Do some of these activities together. Engaging in exhilarating activities can certainly ignite the passion.

Enjoy your own alone time.

21

On the other side of the coin, it's a good idea to spend time away from your partner as well. Everyone needs space at times. Also, time apart can build up the anticipation for some of the things you may have planned with your partner.

Share your goals.

22

Keep an open conversation with your partner about your future plans. Things may not always go according to plan, but it's good to talk about your dreams and goals. While it's fun to discuss what things were like at the beginning of your relationship, it's also enjoyable to discuss where you think things are going.

Surprise your partner with a gift.

23

It doesn't have to be something expensive; in fact, you could even make it yourself. Just explore some thoughtful ideas that will let your partner know that you care about them.

Make a meal together.

24

You can still have a romantic dinner even if you aren't going out. Choose a nice meal that you can cook together. You're probably used to either you or your partner cooking. It'll be a nice change to have the two of you in the kitchen together.

Share memories.

25

Spend some time reflecting on your past. It's always fun to recall the beginnings of your relationship. It doesn't matter if it was months or decades ago. It's a great way to pass the time with your partner.

Deal with conflicts lovingly.

26

Even in healthy relationships, conflicts come up. Sometimes they are for petty reasons and sometimes they are major life-altering problems. Your goal isn't to avoid conflicts at all cost; rather your goal is to develop a way to deal with conflict in a healthy way.

You don't always have to be right or have the last word.

27

Really listen to what your partner is saying even if it isn't what you want to hear. Don't blame each other, it doesn't matter who is at fault. Be open and honest about your thoughts and feelings.

Be open to change.

28

People are constantly changing and evolving. You must be open to change within yourself and your relationship. You may be disappointed by the changes your partner is going through, but that's exactly why you'll need to remain open and understanding.

Act and speak positively about your partner in front of other people.

29

It's easier to trust someone who speaks well of you. Conversely, if someone speaks about you in a nasty way, you're likely to distrust them. If you have something negative to say, try to say at least five positive statements prior to making the negative statement.

Don't go to bed angry.

30

This may be one of the best pieces of advice for any relationship. Instead of going to bed upset and getting up the next day still angry, do whatever you can to resolve any issue that could strain your relationship. This means you'll need to have good problem solving skills but they can be learned. It just takes practice.

31

If arguing is a problem for you and your partner, you can turn the arguments into meaningful discussions with the right techniques. When you need to discuss an issue, set the right stage for effective communication by choosing a time when both of you are calm and in a good mood. Instead of both of you talking at the same time, only one person should be allowed to talk at a time.

Avoid accusations.

32

Blaming or accusing may also be an issue you have with your partner. You can both help alleviate this problem by using "I" messages rather than "you" messages. Starting a statement with "You always" will accomplish one thing and one thing only: you, your partner, or both of you will immediately become defensive.

Physically be there for your partner.

33

Being "there" for someone physically means just what the word implies. You're there for them in person, standing by their side, listening to them, or talking with them so they're not alone. This may be at three in the afternoon, or three in the morning!

Make a CD.

34

Remember mixed tapes when you were a teenager? Technology has advanced a bit since then, so why not create a CD that holds all the songs that have meant something to you and your partner since you've known each other. It will remind you of old times and bring back memories of the past. These are great as gentle reminders of why you love them so much.

When discussing money, try to be business-like, not emotional.

35

Avoid blaming and labeling. Most important, no matter how tight money is, reserve a small amount for pleasure. Even if you go out once a week to a movie or for pizza, just the two of you, you'll feel better about your relationship in general if you indulge yourselves once and a while.

Don't underestimate the power of 'love notes'.

36

Although they are inexpensive and easy to give, love notes are reminders that simply reassure. It is not necessary to be original or even creative with your love notes. These little reminders can be written on cards that accompany a small present or flower, or they may stand alone. When giving a card, try hiding it in a place where your partner will be surprised.

Don't allow negative behavior to rule your love life.

37

When a relationship is strained, it can sink very quickly. Sometimes you don't do what your partner wants you to do, so he/she becomes upset and even distant. Agree to allow each other to make your own choices. Remember, women will respond quickest to a man's action or lack of action. Men will respond quickest to a woman's attitude.

Give genuine gifts!

38

Take the time to pay sincere gifts of love. Offer genuine compliments often. Offer generous praise for your partner. The road to prosperity in your love life will be paved with a commitment to generosity towards your partner.

39

There is great healing in your power of touch. Hold hands. Kiss in your car. Give your partner a massage. Spend time holding and caressing. Give your partner an extended hug every day; one that lasts several minutes. Make the effort to touch each other every day.

Celebrate your love life!

40

Plan for special days in romantic ways. Make a note of very special days. The ones that belong just to the two of you; your first date, when you first made love, when you moved into your home, the day you got married, the day of the proposal. Plan something really special.

41

Kick your heels up and play like a kid again. Tell your partner you want to enjoy what he or she enjoys and then spend the entire day together. Make a commitment to do this regularly.

Dress up and go out on the town.

42

Go on a date and dress to the nines! Make it a special night; even rent a tuxedo or buy a new dress. Make advance reservations for a classy restaurant. Delight in all the planning.

Expect the unexpected.

43

Be spontaneous and suggest something completely out of character. Send an intimate greeting card for no reason. Suddenly stop beside a country road, breath in the fresh air and say, "I love you!" and then be on your way. If your partner loves sports on TV, sit alongside and watch the game, too. Let your imagination have free reign.

Trust and be trusted.

44

Be a straight shooter. Trust is the great equalizer in a good relationship; without it there is no good! A good foundation in a healthy love relationship is built on trust and trust must be earned. Holding back on the truth about how you feel, only telling part of the story, fudging on what your wants and needs are to your partner slowly erodes the trust in your relationship.

Go the extra mile.

45

Motivate each other to be the best you can be. Be inventive in coming up with ways to inspire your love life. Never stop. NEVER! Push the romance envelope with a getaway in the mountains for a long weekend. Splurge and go all out! Use your imagination.

Memories last a lifetime - so can your love life.

46

Create a love scrapbook. Stash your memories of special greeting cards, snapshots, ticket stubs, a handwritten love poem, a funny, thoughtful valentine. Celebrate spending time together living out a life's dream. If you have always wanted to see your favorite band in concert, go! Save the tickets and program and frame them as a lifelong memory the two of you have shared.

Go on a date with your partner.

47

Even relationships that are old-hat need new juice! Once every week plan to spend some quality date time together. If you have kids, enlist a trusted friend to stay the night with them and head for the "ten buck a night motel." Relive those olden days when you really lit the fire.

Have a regular movie night, both in and out.

48

This is the main stay of any romantic couple, so be sure to not neglect this one. So long as you are watching a good variety of interesting flicks, and cuddling up and smooching as you watch the movie together, you are doing just fine! Plan for some yummy snacks!

Have independent interests.

49

You cannot have anything interesting to say if you spend every waking moment doing and experiencing the same things. Having independent interests is not a sign of a weak relationship but rather a sign of its strength. Having independent interests mean that you have something unique to bring to conversations, ensuring that you both have something interesting, and yes exciting, to say to one another.

Be spontaneous.

50

As we grow comfortable in our relationships and more busy by life's obligations, we have a tendency to rely upon the strength of our relationships and in so doing fail to keep things spontaneous. So to mix things up; plan an afternoon or evening event that is completely new. Try that show your partner has been dying to see, or visit that new restaurant that just opened up.

Never threaten separation.

51

This is less a rule to keep things exciting, and more one to keep them sound. A relationship can only grow and remain exciting if both parties are confident in their commitment to one another. As a consequence, make it a rule between you and your partner that you never threaten separation.

Forgive and don't hold grudges.

52

Disagreements are only natural in any relationship. Learning to forgive and not hold grudges is vital if they are to prevent bitterness from seeping in and souring things. People make mistakes and do stupid things. We need to be quick to say sorry, and quick to forgive. Couples must never harbor grudges. Besides, harboring grudges solves nothing.

Be respectful and honest with one another.

53

Don't take one another for granted. Learn to say thank you. Express your appreciation for the things your partner does for you. Tell the truth. If there is a problem talk about it, don't bottle it up. Couples who face their problems and talk things through are the ones that are most likely to build a strong, loving relationship.

Remember to laugh often.

54

The daily grind of life can make everything seem like a chore. Everyone in a relationship should take time to share jokes and other crazy antics to decrease tension. Remember, laughter is healing.

Don't forget to communicate.

55

It may seem obvious, but good communication is the key to a fulfilling relationship. If you are feeling upset by something your partner has said or done you should tell them right away, you shouldn't assume that they will guess what is wrong. What may be obvious to you may not be obvious to them! Your partner too, needs to be more forthcoming in sharing what is on their mind.

Make decisions together.

56

It is important that couples make joint decisions on things. One must not be superior over the other. If you can't reach agreement straight away, leave it for a while and come back to it again later. If there is still a stale mate, be prepared to give in to your partner. Take turns in giving in to one another. Your relationship isn't a competition!

Be predictable, though not boring!

57

Focus on acting predictably if you need to build trust. Be consistent in what you do. This doesn't mean you must be boring. If there is a twinkle in your eye and a dose of spontaneity every so often, for goodness sakes be spontaneous and fun loving. But, be spontaneous consistently! Be true to who you have always been and be that consistently, whoever you tend to be!

Inform your significant other when you become "unpredictable".

58

We all make shifts and changes. Make sure you inform your partner of what you are experiencing! Say, "I really don't know what is going on in me right now, but I'm moving in a different direction. I might do some silly things, but my intent is not to harm you or scare you. Accept some of my wondering and please be there for me? I may need to run some of this by you every so often!"

Make sure your words match the message.

59

Mean what you say and say what you mean. When your partner hears one thing in your words but your tone of voice, body language and facial expressions are really saying something else, you open the relationship to some crazy making days. Which message are they to believe? This can waste a tremendous amount of energy and she learns not to trust part of what you are saying.

Be very very careful of keeping secrets.

60

Even little secrets can be destructive as often your partner will sense something is 'up' yet cannot put their finger on why. When we can't trust the messages that come from within us, we find it very difficult to trust the messages of the other person. Secrets demand tremendous energy and erode trust.

Let your needs be known - loudly.

61

Be a little - no, be a lot - self-centered. (Be self-centered, but not selfish!) Have you ever been around someone who stated clearly what they needed/wanted? Didn't you respect that person? Because you knew where they stood, and therefore where you stood, didn't that interaction move toward a trusting relationship?

State who you really are.

62

Take some time to reflect on your standards. What are your standards for a relationship? What standards do you hold for yourself? What do you order your life around? What are the 4 top values in your life? What are some themes that you live by? What are you known for? And then...begin letting significant people in your life know. They will thank you for the opportunity to know you.

63

Sometimes you need to say no! Often it is crucial to say no! Saying no sets boundaries around you that protect you from being hurt or venturing into territory that will be destructive to your heart and soul. You draw a line. You stop tolerating that which drains energy and makes you less than YOU. You refuse to allow the destructive behaviors of others to destroy you.

Dig into the dirt.

64

Relationships of emotional investment, by their nature, bring trials, tribulations, fears, chaos, change, stretching and growth. They become the foundation from which your life is shaped. Be fearless when faced with turmoil, upset, crisis, questions, and fears. When the time is right, seek them out. Move toward the unknown. Dig into the dirt of your relationship and uncover the treasures.

Know the difference between falling in love and maintaining a loving relationship.

65

Falling in love can often be like being intoxicated, the subject of your love can do no wrong and all different areas of your brain are impaired due to your preoccupation with them. Unfortunately, this state rarely lasts past the first few years, so in many cases it's necessary to work together at maintaining a healthy and loving relationship.

Learn that mending a relationship doesn't mean mending your partner.

66

A relationship includes you both, and so any issues or situations always include both of you. You can't fix things by modifying the behavior of one person; it has to be a team effort. People aren't like animals, and you shouldn't have to "train" your partner into making you happy. It's not fair on them, and it's not fair on you.

Work as a team.

67

Talk to each other and ask what you both need to enlighten yourself out of any stress or other problems. One should support the other by means of understanding everything he or she is going through.

Have your full and endless support for each other.

68

Though some differences may arise on some things that needs a decision, it will be very rewarding if you will support whoever is tasked to make that decision. Respect each other's decision. Be there always for him/her, in achievements and in failure. That support, for sure, will be appreciated.

Show your care for your partner every day of your life.

69

Happy couples do show how much they care for each other. Take him/her out for a dinner, or just find something to do for them that you'll know they'd appreciate. Even the little things can produce large results!

Never bring up mistakes of the past.

70

Whenever something goes wrong, do not rub past issues in. Don't dwell over the past such that you become blind with the wonderful things ahead of your relationship.

At least once every day, try to say one complimentary thing to your partner.

71

When a couple always spends time with each other, they often forget about courtesy. "Take the trash out. Do the laundry." Isn't there something missing in those phrases? Perhaps putting "Please" before each sentence would make it sound so much better. Never take each other for granted.

If you have to disagree, do it lovingly.

72

There will be lots of times when you and your spouse won't agree at all in some aspects. Don't make your point sound like a criticism to your partner. It doesn't matter who is wrong or right. Always bear in mind that an argument doesn't need a winner or a loser.

Listen even if you feel like you've heard the same statement over and over again.

73

Sometimes venting is necessary, and if your partner can't release their mental baggage with you, to whom will they voice their concerns?

Start a ritual just for the two of you.

74

Ideally, you'll both take time out to do it every day or a few times a week. Engaging in ritual behavior, like sharing coffee, watching funny movies together or taking walks, gives you something to look forward to and can help you build intimacy.

Instead of mulling over how to be romantic, simply do it!

75

Romance is in the little gestures. If you spend too much time thinking about it, you will constantly talk yourself out of it. You will worry about rejection, and be afraid that your gesture will go unnoticed. Don't think about it, just do it!

Remember why you love your partner.

76

When things become stale and routine, it's very easy to begin to see your partner as something other than a partner, just someone who lives with you, like a housemate or whatever. This is not a good place for your relationship to be, so if you feel like this sometimes, take a moment to remember what it is about your partner that you love.

Show your partner that you respect them.

77

In a long term relationship, respect is one of the hardest things to get back once it has gone, so it's always worthwhile to show your partner that you respect them. You can show your respect by trying not to be critical about them and their ideas, and always making a point of listening when they speak to you. After a while you'll find that your partner will begin to do the same for you.

A problem shared is a problem halved.

78

If you do have something that's bothering you, even if it directly concerns your partner, you are better off speaking about it with them. You'll usually find that if you don't tell them, things will get a little worse and a little harder for each day that passes.

Live each day as though it were your last.

79

Make sure you say the things you want to say to your partner today and do the things you want to do for them today. Don't hold back a good word or a good deed when you know it can do wonders for your relationship.

Take care of yourself.

80

Make sure that your spiritual, emotional, psychological and physical batteries are charged. If you need to spend some time doing a hobby, visiting with some friends, or pampering yourself, do it! So long as your "me" time is in moderation, you'll feel a lot healthier, and your relationship will reflect it.

Focus on what you like and love about your partner.

81

Forget the negatives. We truly do get more of what we focus on. If you are having problems, begin focusing on the positive in your relationship and not the negative. Most importantly, stop when you start to criticize them. Turn your thinking to what you like about them and begin to see how your relationship gets better.

Kindness matters.

82

Be kind. Very often, people in relationships treat the people closest to them worse than they treat acquaintances or even total strangers. Go the extra step first. This week, do something kind for your partner that you wouldn't normally do and without expectation of anything in return.

Ask for what you want.

83

Most people expect the people who are in relationship with them to be mind readers. If you're expecting others to be psychics, you're in for a painful ride if you're in relationship with them. If you want your needs to be met, you have to tell people what these needs are.

Be willing to risk opening your heart and letting your partner in.

84

We can be in a relationship for many years and still not allow another person to penetrate our walls of protection. If you want to have a relationship that is alive and growing, being willing to risk is a prerequisite.

Don't treat your partner the way you want to be treated!

85

Many couples make the big mistake of treating their partner in the way they wish their spouse would treat them! In other words, smothering your partner in hugs and kisses isn't going to make him/her want to hug/kiss you more if what they actually need from you is "acts of service" like taking out the trash or cleaning the house!

Let your partner influence you.

86

Be willing to share in his/her decisions. Understand his/her goals and when you do not agree at some point, at least support him or her.

Be adventurous in the bedroom.

87

Your sex life should be more than satisfactory. Experimenting is not a bad idea. Make your bed room romps something each one always looks forward to. Do not be critical with each other as well in making love. Learn to appreciate and communicate.

Don't forget that you can still flirt!

88

Why not send a sexy text message or email while you are at work? This reminds the other person that you are thinking about him or her. It also increases the intensity of love so that you actually look forward to seeing each other when you return home from work.

Celebrate all your partner's successes with them.

89

This can be just a high five to a glass of champagne. Whatever the scale of the success calls for, make it a joint celebration. After all...if it's important to them, then it's important to you, too!

Allow yourself to be impressed by your partner.

90

Don't forget to let them know if they do so. 'I'm proud of you' is something that everyone loves being told by someone they care about.

Be aware of which of your expectations your partner meets.

91

Now see if you are willing to be satisfied with that. Sometimes just deciding that what your partner offers is good enough, can allow the love to re-ignite once again. Then, let them know that they're making you happy. Most people have a deep need to know and to hear that they are meaningful to you.

You have to be honest and loyal at all times.

92

If you want your partner to trust you, you should be honest in every way. This does not mean however that you are obliged to tell every detail of what you do during the day. This is just a matter of being truthful when your partner asks you some questions because making up stories or telling lies will not do your relationship any good at all!

93

Good relationships are all about being on the same side. What's the purpose in scoring all those points? Sure you may cross the finish line first today and maybe tomorrow as well. But you'll be all alone when you do, and if you carry on this way, eventually you may not have anyone left in your life to compete with!

Understand a relationship is not about "ownership".

94

Possessiveness and jealousy are two of the most destructive of all human forces. Very few relationships will survive the poison of this twin-horned devil. Let it go!

Learn how to bend, but never so far that you snap.

95

Relationships are all about give and take. It's OK to bend with the wind sometimes. That's the nature of the dance. But it's not OK to bow over so far, so often, and so low, that you get worn down, weaken and snap. Learn how much to give, how much to take, and when to walk away.

A relationship is a partnership, a two way street.

96

Don't assume that it can work with all the effort coming from one side. Don't run, don't try and break free, follow relationship advice that has been tried and tested. Even the little gestures which you know your partner would appreciate can make a huge difference!

Maree Crosbie has over 14 years experience as a Life Coach and Financial Counsellor. During this time she has worked with a wide variety of clients. Maree loves coaching and sees it as an opportunity for her clients to make the very best of their lives and relationships. Maree says that it is an honor to share in peoples' growing confidence and achievements.

Made in the USA
Charleston, SC
24 May 2012